GREAT
ANSWERS
to DIFFICULT
QUESTIONS
about SEX

GREAT ANSWERS to DIFFICULT QUESTIONS about SEX

What Children Need to Know

Linda Goldman

Jessica Kingsley Publishers
London and Philadelphia

First published in 2010
by Jessica Kingsley Publishers
116 Pentonville Road
London N1 9JB, UK
and
400 Market Street, Suite 400
Philadelphia, PA 19106, USA

www.jkp.com

Library of Congress Cataloging in Publication Data
Goldman, Linda, 1946-
    Great answers to difficult questions about sex : what children need to know / Linda Goldman.
        p. cm.
    ISBN 978-1-84905-804-9 (alk. paper)
    1. Sex instruction for children 2. Children and sex I. Title.
    HQ53.G585 2010
    649'.65--dc22
                                                                    2009029335

British Library Cataloguing in Publication Data
A CIP catalogue record for this book is available from the British Library

ISBN 978 1 84905 804 9

Printed and bound in the United States by
Thomson-Shore Inc., 7300 W. Joy Road, Dexter, MI 48130

Contents

Preface

Children are human beings. Human beings are sexual beings.

A newborn child's experience with sexuality begins at birth. A mother's touch, a father's kiss, a warm bath, and a changed diaper are all a part of our children's sexuality. As they grow, girls and boys are naturally curious about themselves and their bodies. Toddlers begin exploring genitals in the bathtub. At some time between the ages of two and three the question "Where did I come from?" emerges. Their minds are innocent, not filled with embarrassment or shame. This makes it simpler to answer questions about sex with confidence and humor.

These dialogues can become a normal part of family life that can begin with labeling body parts, talking about pregnancy, and having a baby. Answering early questions from young children can set a family tone of trust and safety. And by the time a child is older discussions on birth control, abstinence, and sexual activity can be comfortable and relaxed.

By the age of five children are faced with media bombardment and peer information as they enter a larger world of school. It is essential that adults give young people the right information about sex to balance the gross and faulty perceptions they are inundated with. Letting young people know the scientific facts about sex and reproduction helps replace incorrect ideas from peers and media.

Talking about private parts of the body and the importance of telling if something is uncomfortable helps them feel safe. The sooner in life children can come to adults to talk about sex and love and relationships the better they will feel about continuing the discussion as they mature. This beginning prepares them for openness as they become more sexually active.

An unfolding process

Answering children's questions about sex is an unfolding process. There is no perfect time to sit and discuss "the birds and the bees." There is no perfect age to have "the sex talk." The topic of sexuality and gender issues is an ongoing learning experience that begins at birth and continues and builds over time. Educating girls and boys on sex begins long before they enter school. Children explore their bodies as toddlers and pre-schoolers. Using their natural instincts and curiosity, this normal and healthy discovery grows and expands as they develop.

Talking about the actual "birds and bees" can be a safe conversation for the young child. Pictures, conversations, and contact with animals are often easier and more natural for parents as well as children. If talking about sex progresses to humans too soon some adults become nervous and inhibited. Beginning in the simplest way can set the stage for evolving dialogues.

Understanding the value of children's questions is essential. These questions guide caring adults into the child's inner world by signaling what they are thinking and feeling. One ten-year-old girl was having difficulty sleeping. She seemed to be worrying a lot. Embarrassed and shy, she stuffed what was bothering her deep inside until she could hold it in no longer.

As her mom was tucking her into bed, she began to sob and sob. "Mom, can I get pregnant if I kiss a boy?" What a relief she felt to get it out and realize her mother was more than willing to respond. "Why do you ask?" Mom replied. "What do you think?" "I kissed a boy and my friends said I could have a baby. *Is that true?*" she whispered and relapsed into tears. This parent's reflection of her daughter's question and then finding out more information allowed a deeper insight into what was troubling her child. A simple statement of "No, that isn't true," created instant relief and kept the door open for future talks about sex, intimacy, and growing up.

Finding the right words

Often parents feel ill equipped to talk to children about sex. The challenge of finding the right words that allow the flow of ideas without embarrassment and minimization is not an easy task. Many of us grew up in an age when the subject of sex was not discussed and no role models for dialogue were present. One mother told us the topic of sex was never discussed when she was a child. When she was 11 her mother left a book by her bed about the facts of life and love. Not a word was ever spoken about it.

Today our children live in a different world. They are inundated with sexuality through movies, videos, friends, and computer games. They can instantaneously see graphic images about sex and gender issues or read and hear information with the click of a mouse or TV remote. PG 13 films seem almost X-rated to an older generation.

One seven-year-old came home from school and asked, "Mom, do I look hot?" Her mother automatically responded, "Maybe. Why don't you take off your sweater." "No, Mom," she insisted. "Do I look hot? My friend said I look hot today." Mom gasped as she realized the question was not what she thought it was, and then explained "hot" was a word that meant sexy and was for much older girls and women. She told her daughter she looked pretty and sweet that day. Having real conversations can serve as guides to right action and safeguards to re-frame misconceptions gleaned from the media or peers.

Parents must be prepared to initiate and promote dialogue in this twenty-first-century environment of exposure to delicate and important subjects involving sex and gender issues – beginning at even very early ages. Young people are more sophisticated and savvy than previous generations and deserve appropriate and accurate information.

How much is too much

Many times adults ponder and ponder the "right" answer to questions about such a sensitive topic as sex. They feel inadequate to know the correct terminology for discussion and the appropriate way to present it. Frequently they tend to give lengthy explanations to simple questions when children are usually satisfied with short, honest answers. If kids want to know more they will usually let you know.

Parents worry that their children may bring up the subject of sex and they will be unprepared to answer their questions. They may feel self-conscious about responding. This often leads to clichés that can inhibit true understanding and confuse the truth. Hastily answering a child's question "Where do babies come from?" by speedily spurting out the cliché "of course, from storks" not only creates a myth to be dispelled, but the possibility of that child's losing trust or not believing future responses. Instead, with honest feedback children will see the adults around them as a trustworthy source of sexual information.

The complexities of a child's conversation may depend on their maturity, curiosity, and developmental stage. Children respond in many ways. For one child a simple answer is sufficient. Too much detail can be overwhelming, with information he or she may just not be ready to understand. Another child may jump into the next set of questions on a deeper level.

Adults and children have very different concepts of sex. The grown-up mind might immediately rush to sexual intercourse or explicit definitions of body parts as an explanation. A child's may not be thinking about that at all. A five-year-old asked his mom, "How can you tell if a baby is a boy or a girl?" Mom nervously pondered what to respond but instead asked the question "What do you think?" "By their name, of course," was the little boy's logical response.

Honoring children's questions

Listen carefully to your child's questions. Allow children to become the expert in where they are in their search for understanding sex and sexuality.

Honoring children's questions about sex and sexuality is important. These questions then provide insight into their inner thoughts and feelings. How much you tell young people depends on their question and level of understanding and your own comfort with the subject. Adults must be prepared to talk with children over and over again as they develop and their questioning reappears at increasing levels of sophistication. No question is wrong and no answer is perfect. The goal of this resource is to guide parents and other caring adults towards actively encouraging children's questions, and to enable adults to become comfortable and creative in their responses. For so many adults who have difficulty in finding those "right" words to respond, this book offers some suggestions.

The following chapters present simple and usable language for conversation. The chapters' examples of sub-questions from children of different age groups will compose the framework of discussion. Genuine age-appropriate vocabulary and practical, simple guides for discussion can help eliminate fear and create a healthy dialogue with children for successfully embracing the delicate, yet important, topic of sex.

CHAPTER 1

Where do babies come from? How do they grow?

Young children will often surprise parents with an unexpected, seemingly random question such as "Where do babies come from?" This question may be asked at an inconvenient or awkward time when adults may respond in a limited or embarrassed way. Even the youngest of children can understand it takes a mom and a dad to make a baby. If adults respond with teasing or innuendos instead of facts, half-truths and myths become more difficult to undo.

Laying the foundation with a simple and honest explanation plants the seeds of truth to build larger concepts later. In the following case study, a child creates a challenge for his mother in the grocery store. Although at the time he didn't appear to fully integrate his mother's response, it serves as a building block for future discussion.

Tyler (5): a case study

Tyler was five years old and very curious. He questioned his mother Janet about everything. Why is the sky blue? Where does the sun go at night? What is ice cream made of? His inquisitive mind explored all areas and conversations. Mom never knew when the next question would come. She certainly hadn't expected this one standing in line at the grocery store – while they were waiting next to a mom with her baby.

"Hey, Mom," he said in a loud voice, "Where do babies come from anyway?" Silence filled the air. Stunned, his mother recoiled as the rest of the shoppers looked to her for the answer.

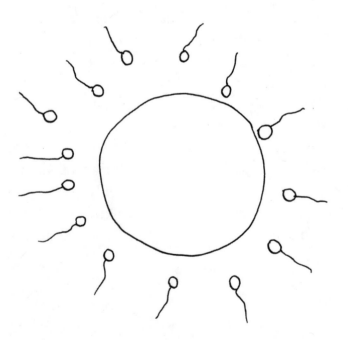

Janet and her husband Charlie had discussed on countless nights the importance of answering Tyler's questions, but she wasn't prepared for this scenario. "Seize the moment," Charlie would say, "and answer his questions right away." With this advice in mind, Janet took a deep breath and bravely did her best. "The mom and dad make a baby. You grew inside my belly in a place called a uterus." Tyler stopped in his tracks, took a minute to think, and then responded. "That's the most ridiculous thing I ever heard."

I don't believe my mom. Where do babies really come from?
Babies really grow inside their mothers. It's a special place called a uterus or womb.

Greg (11) Tyler's older brother

I do believe my mom. I know babies grow inside their mother. But where do they come from?
A woman and a man make a baby together. A sperm from a man's body and an egg from a woman's body come together. When parents want to have a baby they come together in a very special way called making love or having sex. Their bodies are so close the man's penis fits inside the woman's vagina. The sperm from the man goes from his penis to meet the egg inside the woman. When the sperm and an egg join together it is called fertilization. Then the baby begins to grow and develop.

How do they join together?

The sperm cells leave the tip of the dad's penis and swim into the mom's vagina and through her uterus into two tubes called fallopian tubes. When the sperm and egg join in the fallopian tube something miraculous happens, the cells come together and a beginning baby or embryo starts to grow.

Suppose the sperm and the egg can't join, then what happens?

Sometimes a family can't have a baby because their sperm and egg don't join or fertilize, or because there is no sperm or egg. That's called being infertile, because two people can't fertilize an egg with a sperm. Then doctors help to put a sperm and egg together in the hospital and place the fertilized egg in the women's uterus to grow a baby.

Can children make babies?

No, they are too young. The necessary cells, the sperm cells and egg cells, don't start to be made in your body until we get to be young adults – that's called puberty. Then they can join together to make a baby.

Can two moms or two dads have babies?

There are many ways to create a family and have children. Sometimes a mom and dad, two moms, or two dads decide to adopt a baby because they are not able to get pregnant. They bring a baby from another family into their home and raise that baby as their own. Two moms, two dads, or a mom and dad can all be good parents. Being a good parent is showing love and caring for your children.

Allie (7)

My mom said she loved me so much she traded her new computer for me? Is that where I came from?

No, it's not. Your mom made a joke about where babies come from. Sometimes grown-ups make jokes instead of explaining where babies come from. They may think you are too young to understand. But jokes can be confusing, and giving the facts helps to understand. You came from a place inside your mom called a uterus. That is where babies come from.

Tommy (9)

My dad said Mom ate some seeds to have a baby. Is that true?

No. That is not true. Your dad was just telling a funny story. I can clear that idea up for you. It takes an egg and a sperm to make a baby.

It looks like my mom has a baby in her tummy. But how does it start to grow?

That's a really good question. Your mom and dad wanted to have a baby and were glad to have you and now wanted another child. It takes a man and a woman to make a baby. The man has something called a sperm and the woman has an egg that stays inside of her in a place called a uterus or womb. This is a special place near Mom's stomach, but not in her stomach. The uterus is where the baby grows. The man's sperm and the woman's egg join together to begin growing a baby. This beginning baby is called an embryo.

What is an embryo?

An embryo is a group of cells that grow to become a baby. The embryo grows inside the lining of a mom's uterus. After three months the growing baby is called a fetus. It takes nine months for the fetus to be ready to be born a baby.

I'm so glad you asked about the baby. If you have any more questions about this or anything else, let me know. I am happy to answer.

Does the baby keep growing inside Mom?

Yes, after the egg and sperm come together they form the beginning baby called an embryo and then a fetus. The fetus stays warm and safe floating in a sac filled with warm water called the amniotic sac. The growing fetus stays protected while it grows into a full-size baby.

Can the fetus eat or drink while it is inside?

That's a great question. It does both. The fetus might drink some of the water in the amniotic sac. Or it may get nutrition from the same foods Mom eats. Mom breathes and eats for herself and for the baby. Blood carries the air and food through a part of Mom's uterus called a placenta and it goes through a cord called the umbilical cord into the baby's body.

When a baby is born the umbilical cord is cut and then children have a belly button or navel. That is the place where the umbilical cord was attached to you when you were inside Mom.

I think they get bored.
What can a fetus do while it is growing?

It can do lots of things. Beside eating and drinking, it can kick and squirm and even hiccup and burp. If you put your hand on a pregnant mom's tummy you might feel the fetus moving. It is very exciting. Sometimes you can even see their elbows or fists make bumps in Mom's tummy.

Growing babies can suck their thumbs, stretch their bodies, or even open their eyes under water. They can take naps too.

Can I see the baby inside my mom's belly?

Yes, it is amazing. Now the doctors can take a picture of the developing baby. It is called an ultrasound picture.

What is an ultrasound?

An ultrasound is a moving picture of the baby. At the very moment it is being taken it appears on a screen sort of like a fuzzy television. Sometimes the doctors can tell from this picture if the baby is a girl or a boy. They might see the heartbeat or parts of the baby's body. They can check to see if the baby is healthy inside their mother.

The ultrasound can even show if there are two or three babies inside. And you can listen to the baby's heart beating!

The nurse can give you a photo of the baby to take home. This is really the first baby picture.

Concluding thoughts

Children want to know the place where babies come from, how they get out, and how they are made. Some parents say heaven, others say the stork, the mailman, and even the computer store.

The expedience of offering a distorted cliché can help adults avoid the embarrassment of explanation for the moment. It diffuses their worry that they will say the wrong thing or disintegrate on the spot rather than face a child's question. But when one begins with a distortion with children, it can only lead to confusion and possibly lack of trust until it is corrected.

If adults aren't sure what to say, they can take "time to think" before answering a difficult question. A good response to uncertainty can be "That is a great question. I need time to think about the answer. Let's talk about it later." This allows for the opportunity to prepare a meaningful response without pressure.

CHAPTER 2

How did I get in my mom's tummy? How did I get out? What does pregnant mean?

When adults answer in a simple and straightforward manner, young children are usually satisfied. Many of us as adults have a background that makes it uncomfortable to discuss sex with our children. Responding at the time of the question is essential, as children resonate with answers appropriate for specific developmental stages of learning. Sometimes parents and educators fear too much information may be harmful, but no response or too limited a response can inhibit future inquisitiveness.

Usually girls and boys will absorb answers that are meaningful and become bored if they are overloaded with information. Children not only are curious about where they came from but also may wonder and worry about the birth process itself. "How do babies get out?" may be a natural segue to finding out they came from being inside their mother's uterus. Then their growing interest in the subject might peak with wonderment about conception as they might ask, "What caused me to happen in the first place?"

David (6): a case study

David's mom was pregnant and soon to have a baby. Her tummy had become huge and David had watched it grow and grow for nine months. Dad said the baby was coming soon. David knew his new brother or sister was growing inside his mom but he couldn't figure out how the baby could get out. His friend Tommy said the stork delivered the baby. Joey said the angels bring the baby from heaven. But David didn't believe them. He told his dad, "My new baby has to get out of my mom's body. Her tummy is getting so big I am afraid it is going to burst like a balloon. But I'm worried. How will it happen?"

How are babies born?

When a baby is ready to be born, doctors and nurses help the baby and mother. Muscles inside the mom's uterus begin to contract. This helps her to push the baby through the vagina. The tightening of these muscles is called having a contraction.

Is the baby really inside my mom's stomach?

No, the baby is not in your mom's stomach. It is growing in a place inside her called a uterus or womb, which is underneath Mom's stomach. Food, not babies, go in stomachs. The uterus is a safe place inside mothers where babies can grow.

But how does the baby get out?

When the baby is ready to be born, it comes out of a place inside Mom called a vagina. The vagina is the birth passage that the baby comes through. Usually the mom pushes the baby out of her vagina. It's made in a special way so that it can stretch wide enough to let the baby slide out when the time is right.

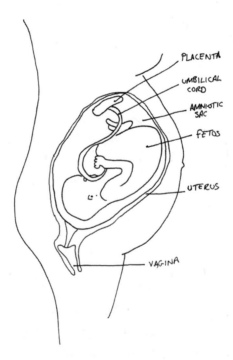

PLACENTA

UMBILICAL CORD

AMNIOTIC SAC

FETUS

UTERUS

VAGINA

Is that the only way?

No, sometimes moms need to have an operation in the hospital for the baby to be able to come out. This is called a cesarean birth or a C-section. The doctor gives Mom medicine to take away any pain so this won't hurt. The doctor cuts through Mom's skin into her uterus to bring the baby out. The doctor takes the baby out and announces if it is a boy or girl. When the baby is out the doctor sews stitches to close up where the cut was and Mom can begin to heal. A baby is born.

What is the first thing the new baby does?

Usually the new baby begins to cry. That signals it is breathing on its own. It also lets the doctors know they can cut the cord that attached the baby to its mom. Blood traveled through the umbilical cord to give the baby food and air. Now the baby doesn't need the cord any more. The belly button is where the cord was attached to the baby.

Does it hurt to cut the cord?

No, it doesn't hurt at all. The mom and the baby don't feel any pain. They are fine.

Then what happens?

Then everyone is happy. They can kiss and hug the baby. Sometimes people laugh and sometimes they cry. It is a really special moment when a baby is born.

Why is it so special?

Because you are special. There is only *one* you!

The time you were born becomes your birth date. The hospital records the day, the year, and even the minute you were born. It is your own special time and day and you can celebrate that moment of birth every year.

Where is the baby born?

Sometimes babies are born at home and sometimes at the hospital. Whether at home or in a hospital, usually helpers are there. Dad or a partner can be a helper. A relative like a grandparent or a good friend can help too.

Erin (10)

My mother said she was pregnant and I was growing inside of her and then I was born. What does pregnant mean?

Pregnant means a baby is growing inside the mother. Pregnancy begins with an egg and sperm coming together to form an embryo. Then the baby grows into a fetus. Pregnancy ends when the baby is born.

How do the sperm and egg get together?

Lots of sperm swim through the vagina like tadpoles until one pushes inside an egg. Then an egg shuts closed and no more sperm can come in. The tail falls off the sperm and lots of cells begin to form in a ball. This ball becomes the beginning of a baby and we can say Mom is pregnant.

Are there any other ways to get pregnant?

Yes, there are a few. One way is called in vitro fertilization (IVF). The egg from one woman's ovaries can be taken by a doctor and put in a tiny glass bowl with the sperm from a man. The egg and sperm join to fertilize the egg and then the doctor puts it back into the mother's uterus. It begins to grow into a new baby and the woman is pregnant.

Alternative or artificial insemination is another way to start a pregnancy. Sperm from a man is kept at a hospital or doctor's office. When a woman is ready, the doctor can place the sperm inside her uterus using a syringe. When the sperm fertilizes the egg a new baby begins to grow and the woman is pregnant.

But where does the baby start?

It starts in the mom's uterus. Another word for uterus is womb. The beginning baby grows inside the womb until it is fully developed and is ready to be born.

How long does that take?

It takes around nine months for a baby to become full grown and ready to be born.

Did I look like me when I was born?

Not at the beginning. You started out as an embryo. As the cells grew and matured you began looking like a baby. You grew for nine months inside your mom. You slowly developed all of your body parts as you grew and turned into baby Erin when you were born.

Concluding thoughts

Beginning conversations with children about pregnancy and birth by using age-appropriate facts can clear the way for honest and meaningful dialogues in the future. Young children's fears about where babies come from and if being born hurts can easily be addressed and clarified.

Using clear conversation and preparing appropriate responses ahead of time can avoid the discomfort of being put on the spot or giving misinformation. Welcoming questions without embarrassment and keeping to age-appropriate concepts sets the stage for fluid and continuous dialogues. Using teachable moments such as a pregnant relative or a TV show can be a catalyst for conversation and an assurance that birth and pregnancy are natural processes that children don't need to fear.

CHAPTER 3

How are girls' and boys' bodies alike and different? What are the names of the different body parts for boys and girls?

Talking to children using real words and appropriate labels can begin with our newborn. As we wash them and name body parts such as eyes, toes, and nose, we can also include "let me wash your penis" or "let's wash your vagina" as a natural part of conversation. In this way young children learn proper language for discussing body parts without the overlay of adult embarrassment. This discussion evolves as children mature and need to have more factual conversations on the subjects involving sex. Honest terminology lays the framework for building future dialogues within a fluid and accepting environment.

Questions about sexual or gender issues can sometimes be difficult for adults. Too often children are brought up with slang words for genitals like "willy," "wee-wee," "twinkle," or simply "down there" instead of starting at the beginning with penis or vagina. An adult's avoidance of accurate anatomical terms can communicate a sense of their own discomfort with issues pertaining to sex and give that subliminal message to the child. Responding with inappropriate euphemisms may create confusion when other adults don't know what those words symbolize. One little girl went to school and complained to her teacher, "My 'gee gee' hurts." Her teacher began to laugh a little nervously, not being sure what she meant.

This slang use of vagina can get in the way of a healthy dialogue. Teaching a child to use real terminology enables him to have an open discussion. "A boy at school hit my penis and it hurts," a first grader spontaneously blurted out to his teacher. His comfort with the word penis allowed him to use it without thinking. When parents and children are comfortable with words like penis, vagina, and uterus they build the foundation for generating an engaging dialogue on how these parts work. Using proper terms provides clear language for communication.

Hank (6): a case study

Eight-year-old Tucker loved the Jones's dog Harley that lived next door. Sometimes he would visit Harley and give him a big hug. He would play ball with him a lot and even let Harley lick his face. One time Harley stopped chasing the ball and urinated on a near-by bush. Tucker was shocked and yelled out to his mom, "Mom, Mom, look at Harley's 'wee-wee' sticking out." Tucker's mom wasn't sure but thought he meant penis. She decided to use the real word with Tucker. "That's Harley's penis," she correctly responded. "Oh, that's what it is," said Tucker, as he threw the ball to Harley again.

Tucker's little brother Hank was listening. Hank ran over to Mom and asked:

What's a "wee-wee"?

A "wee-wee" is a made-up name for a boy's penis. Sometimes people have funny names for body parts that are private.

What is a private part?

A private part is part of your body that is covered by your underwear. Sometimes the male parts of a boy's body and the female parts of a girl's body are called private parts.

What are the real names for private parts for boys?

Boys' private parts or genitals are a penis and scrotum. Boys have a penis and they use it to urinate. Your urine collects in a bag inside your body that is called a bladder. The urethra is a tube that comes from your bladder and goes through your penis so that urine can come out. Boys have a scrotum too.

What's a scrotum?

A scrotum is a round sac under your penis. Soft balls called testicles are inside the sac. Testicles eventually make sperm to have babies when you are grown-up.

Will my body change as I get older?

As you get older your private parts grow too. Your penis and testicles get bigger, and eventually testicles will produce sperm.

Mathew (5)

Sometimes I worry I can lose my penis. Can I lose my penis?

No, your penis is a part of your body. You cannot lose it.

Can girls get penises?

No, their bodies are different. They have private parts inside them called a vagina.

Sasha (10): a case study

Sometimes parental awkwardness can even result in chastising a child for proper word use. Ten-year-old Sasha was eating supper with her family when a lively debate ensued about the future. Her brother Andy said a day will come when people will imagine going somewhere and then they will really travel there by thinking about it. Mom said "Never" and Dad said, "You never know." Sasha quickly chimed in, "I'll believe that when girls grow penises." She thought the idea was so funny she couldn't stop laughing. Her mother had the opposite reaction. "What did you say? Don't you ever use that word at the dinner table! Go to your room, young lady."

Sasha was stunned. What had she done wrong? "I was only joking," she thought to herself as she left the room. "What's wrong with the word penis?"

What's wrong with the word penis?
Nothing. It is the real name for a boy's genitals.

What does genitals mean?
Genitals are your sexual organs. They are the penis, scrotum, and testicles on boys and the vulva, vagina, and clitoris on girls.

Do boys and girls have body parts that are the same?
Of course they do! If you look in the mirror with your little brother Georgie you can see you both have heads, necks, arms, legs, noses, teeth, eyes, ears, toes, and fingers. There are other body parts that are the same. Both girls and boys have a bladder and a urethra. The urethra is a tube that allows the urine to go outside of the body.

I helped my mom give my little brother Georgie a bath. Why don't I have one of those – you know?
I think you mean why does Georgie have a penis and you don't.

Yeah. Why doesn't everybody have a penis?

Boys and girls are made differently. Boys have a penis and a scrotum and girls have a vulva, vagina, and a clitoris.

Maggie (8)

What genitals do girls have?

Girls have a vulva, a clitoris, and a vagina.

What is a vulva?

A vulva is the area of soft skin between your legs.

What is a clitoris?

A clitoris is inside the vulva. It is a small piece of skin.

What is a vagina?

It is a passageway inside your body behind your vulva.

Do girls urinate through their vagina?

No, girls urinate through the urethra, which empties out of the body though an opening located just in front of the vagina.

Why do women have hair down there and little girls don't?

Our bodies change as we grow up. Girls begin to grow hair near their vaginas and boys begin to grow hair near their penises. When girls become women, a part of their body inside of them will begin to make little eggs that can become a baby one day.

Why do boys and girls pee in a different way?

That's a good question and lots of children ask it. Another word for pee is urinate. Boys and girls urinate in a different way because their bodies are different and work in different ways, although both have a bladder and a urethra. A boy's urethra brings urine to the tip of their penis. They can sit or even stand up and aim their penis to send urine into the toilet.

Girls sit on the toilet. Their urethra carries urine to an opening right inside the vulva. The vulva covers the opening to the urethra. The urethra is a tube inside a girl's body that lets the urine come through when they are sitting down.

Concluding thoughts

Although most of us are uneasy with proper terminology, it is important to present it as early as possible. Being honest with children, we can still support the open environment we aspire to have. Give children as much information as you feel they can handle while keeping the door open for continuing questions and ongoing dialogue. Sometimes conversations will be repeated several times as children digest and integrate words and meanings. Children will ask more involved questions as they mature, and we need to be prepared to respond with age-appropriate realistic answers.

Children need clear and simple language when speaking about issues involving sex or body parts. All too often adults diminish their knowing by substituting fake words to alleviate being uncomfortable in discussing the topics. "Wiener," "willy," "wee-wee," "down there," etc. avoids real terms like penis and vagina. Children are OK with these words if parents are. Using correct names for body parts creates clear and respectful conversations with a caveat of respect for children of all ages.

Pre-school children can become comfortable with the correct anatomical words. Creating a continuous flow of information can begin with babies. Labeling body parts like head and knee can lead to using actual names such as penis and vagina that helps create direct conversation instead of embarrassment from juvenile labels. This education continues throughout childhood and adolescence.

CHAPTER 4

What parts of my body are private? Why?

Sex education can begin at any time, and adults can be mindful of that at early ages. Infants and toddlers are naturally inquisitive and begin exploration of body parts in a natural way. This can serve as a teachable moment to begin the ongoing open interchange about sex education. Pre-schoolers and older children are curious and they can set the pace with their questions about what they are becoming aware of and want to know. Toddlers will touch themselves in the bathtub or while being diapered without inhibition. How adults respond sets the tone for acceptance.

Young children begin to learn about their bodies and ask questions about their bodies and yours. Respond with respect. Even if nervous laughter feels imminent, try to remain composed and answer questions honestly. Embarrassment will dissipate as direct conversations evolve. Feeling awkward in the beginning can be transformed into a confidence that is part of the job of an adult to responsibly answer children's questions. These questions are healthy and normal.

Lilly (7): a case study

Lilly was seven years old when her mother noticed that she liked to rub herself against her favorite doll. It seemed to be a frequent pastime and as her mother watched she saw Lilly almost get excited when she was doing this. Not sure if this was something natural, Lilly's mother asked the pediatrician about it. He explained many children self-stimulate and suggested Lilly should understand this was normal to do as a private activity. He suggested comparing it to urinating as a natural but private body function.

Mom talked to Lilly and explained this was okay to do and that it would be a good idea to be in her bedroom. Lilly said fine.

A few days later Lilly was taking a bath. Mom came in to help her wash her hair and Lilly began chatting.

What are private parts?

The parts of your body that are covered by your underwear or bathing suit are your private parts.

Is it OK for me to touch my private parts?

Of course it is. It is a part of your body. It is natural for children to be interested in their bodies.

Sometimes touching myself feels good. Is that OK?

Yes, it is fine. Lots of children like to touch or rub themselves and it makes them feel good. Many adults like to touch themselves privately too. Touching yourself can feel good to children and adults, and is called masturbation.

Why do I have to touch myself in private?

In our culture people stay dressed when they are out with friends and family. Being private allows you to have this activity without being disturbed or disturbing others.

Can other people touch my private parts?

Sometimes they can and sometimes they can't. When you go for a check up the doctor or nurse might need to touch a private part to make sure you are healthy. Your parent is with you. That is OK touching. Adults should not be touching a child's private parts.

What should I do if that happens?

Say *Stop!!! I don't want you to do that.*

If they don't listen, tell a grown-up you trust. Even if it is a family friend or someone in your family you must tell another grown-up to make them stop. It is wrong for someone to touch your private parts. Say *no.* If someone says you are a bad child for saying no tell him or her, "I don't believe you!" If you feel uncomfortable, run away.

If they tell you that touches are supposed to be a secret, say no again. Don't keep touches a secret.

Sam (5)

I was playing doctor with Max. We took our clothes off. We heard Mom come in the front door and didn't know what to do. Is it OK to play doctor?

Children are naturally interested in how their bodies and different bodies are made. They like to see how alike or different they are and sometimes want to experiment with touching or seeing each other. Sometimes children like to find out about boys' body parts and girls' body parts. You don't ever need to feel like you have to do something like get undressed or be touched.

You and Max can still play doctor with your clothes on too. If you want to you can read books about how people's and animals' bodies are made and even draw pictures about it. You can also do other things together. You both love to build with blocks. You could make a cool building together too.

What do I do if Max wants to touch my body and I don't want him to?

You can say no to Max and tell him you don't want him to do that. Your body is private. You have the right to privacy. We keep our clothes on when we have company. If you want to learn more your mom or dad can read you the book *My Body is Private* by Linda Girard (see Appendix 3: Useful websites and resources).

Eve (11)

Suppose an adult touches me in my private parts. What should I do?

Say no and tell a grown-up. Adults are not allowed to touch children in their private parts, whether it feels good or not.

Suppose that person won't stop?

If someone wouldn't listen to you, don't be afraid to tell another adult. You would need to keep talking and telling adults until someone listens and makes that person stop. It is not right for an adult to touch children's private parts, except for things like supervised medical exams.

Suppose someone touches me and I don't want him or her to. What can I do?

Tell me or another adult you trust. Don't keep it to yourself. Your body is your own and you have the right to keep it private. No one should ever touch you if you don't want to be touched and you should tell the person to stop it and tell a grown-up. I hope you would tell me right away if this ever happens.

What is a good touch?

A good touch can be a hug or kiss that feels just right to you. A good touch can be when you like to hold a friend's hand or wrestle with your brother.

Suppose I like to touch my private parts. Is that OK?

Yes, it is OK and natural. Children like to explore their bodies, even their genitals or private parts. When we touch our private parts and it gives us pleasure it is called masturbation. It is a natural, normal, and private thing to do. Both girls and boys might like to masturbate because it feels good to them. Some children don't do it at all or only do it rarely. Masturbation is a very private thing to do when you are finding out about your body.

Concluding thoughts

By the age of three or four children realize girls and boys have different body parts. "Playing doctor" is natural for many children as they begin to experiment and explore themselves and others. This sex play can include examining their sexual organs and those of others. For young children this can be harmless, yet placing limits and understanding is important.

Young children also naturally self-stimulate or masturbate. This is a way they express their sexual curiosity. Girls may rub their external genitalia and boys may pull or hold their penis. Remind children that they should not do this in public because it is a private activity. If a child exhibits a need to excessively stimulate himself or herself it may be a signal of anxiety and in some cases sexual abuse. It could be a good idea to consult a physician under these circumstances as it could indicate a physical or emotional problem.

CHAPTER 5

What is sex?

A child's sexual experiences begin at birth, very much before any intellectual questions can be posed. Being held, kissed, bathed, and hugged are the seeds of interest in sexuality. A mother's touch or a dad's tender rocking kindles interest that develops into genital exploration and self-stimulation. Toilet training is a milestone where young children can feel some control over bodily functions.

Parental attitudes about sex and nudity greatly influence their children. Reasonable openness with nudity can create a comfort zone for questions on this natural topic. A feeling of discomfort diminishes as adults become more familiar with questions and answers. Children need valid responses to hold against distorted media representation and peer pressure as they mature. Including the importance of love, intimacy, caring, and respect is essential on any topic and explanation involving reproduction and sexuality.

Secrecy and shame surrounding the word sex can only transfer to children and create more secrecy and shame. Sometimes humor serves as a powerful tool to use in forming a comfort zone around issues involving sex.

When a six-year-old spontaneously blurts out a joke about sex at a family dinner, greeting it with a chuckle and an appropriate response instead of a hushed silence signals a relaxed family tone on the subject. What could have been an uncomfortable situation is transformed into a scenario that becomes an unforgettable humorous moment in time and a valuable teachable tool as well.

Nick (9): a case study

Nine-year-old Nick was precocious in many ways and often his questions seemed far beyond his biological age. After a delicious dinner of spaghetti and homemade apple pie he decided to go upstairs and begin his homework. A half-hour later Mom and Dad were relaxing in the living room when they heard Nick yell down a surprising question: "What does sex mean?"

This question resounded throughout the house. Nick ran downstairs and waited for the answer. Dad began an eloquent and detailed response about "the birds and bees" with a pretty detailed account of making love and what that was about. The conversation took quite some time and Nick listened intently.

When Dad was finished Nick looked at him with puzzlement. "But what does sex mean?"

After all that explanation Dad responded, "I don't know what you are talking about." Nick handed his father an application he was filling out for a school project. It said the word SEX with an F or M next to it. "What does sex mean?"

What does sex mean?

Nick, in the way you asked the question sex means gender or whether you are a boy or a girl – male or female. That is one meaning for sex.

What else is sex?

We can think of sex in lots of ways. It can mean loving, caring, and touching another person. Sexual intercourse, sometimes called "making love," is a kind of sharing or being close between two people. Sexual intercourse can also be about making a baby. When a man puts his penis inside a woman's vagina, it can begin a pregnancy.

I didn't expect that answer. I'll never do that. When I love someone I'll just buy them a present to show how much I love them.

When people love each other they do like to buy presents for each other. That is a way to show caring. Sex can show love and caring too.

It isn't worth it. I don't understand why anyone would do that for someone they love. It's disgusting.

You might change your mind one day. Sex can be a very unique and private way that couples hug, kiss, and hold each other that feels good.

I don't think so. Did you and Dad do that?

Yes, we did. That's how you got here. That is a way we showed each other our love.

Harry (6): a case study

Harry was at a family birthday party with all of his aunts and uncles and cousins. They were celebrating his sister Angie's birthday. Everyone was eating ice cream and cake when Uncle Jack whispered too loudly in Aunt Helen's ear "You look pretty sexy today." Grandma poked him hard. With a menacing scowl on her face, she admonished him in front of everyone. "Don't say the word sex in front of the children!" It was too late. Angie and Harry heard the word sex and didn't know what to think. "Is it a bad word? Will you punish me for saying sex? Why is everybody whispering or angry about it?"

Fortunately Harry's dad stepped in and saved the day. "It's OK, Grandma. Harry and Angie have heard the word sex. They know it means a boy or a girl or something moms and dads do together when they love each other. Uncle Jack is just telling Aunt Helen he likes the way she looks. So do I."

A few weeks later Mom and Dad were getting ready to go to a party. Mom got all dressed up and looked terrific. As she was leaving, Harry yelled to her from across the room, "Hey Mom, you look really sexy." Everyone turned to Harry with shocked expressions. Harry wondered, "Is sex a bad word?"

Is sex a bad word?

No, it is not a bad word.

What is sex?

Sex is a very special, loving, and intimate way grown-ups kiss and touch each other. Couples hold each other in this close and private way. Sometimes that's the way they make a baby.

What does sexy really mean?

It means a man or woman looks a certain way that is attractive to another person.

Tess (11)

My friend Alice is 13. She says she likes to look sexy. She wears tight skirts, makeup, and push up bras. She looks like a TV commercial. Do I have to look sexy too?

No, you are very young and you look beautiful the way you are. It can feel like a lot of pressure to look too grown-up and pretend to be older than you are. People advertise on TV to get children your age to buy their products. They use sex to get you to buy certain jeans or listen to music. They make you feel you will fit in and be popular if you do. They want to make money on what you buy.

But I do want to fit in. Should I buy makeup and tight dresses?

Be yourself. Find friends who like you just like you are and like to do the things you like to do. You have lots of time to be grown-up. I know it's hard when you feel pressured by friends and want to fit into a group. But the best thing is to know who you are and be true to yourself.

Some of my older friends have sex. They say it is safe sex. What is safe sex?

Safe sex refers to protected sex. If a man wears a latex condom that covers his penis during intercourse, it can help stop the woman from getting pregnant. It also helps protect him and his partner from diseases or infections that can be transmitted during sexual intercourse. These diseases and infections transmitted during sexual contact from one person to another are called sexually transmitted diseases (STDs) or sexually transmitted infections (STIs). One of these sexually transmitted diseases is HIV. The condom helps protect him and his partner from giving or getting HIV and helps make sex safer from getting other diseases, infections, or an unwanted pregnancy, but even condoms are not 100 percent reliable as protection.

What is HIV?

HIV is an infection and one of several sexually transmitted diseases (STDs). HIV stands for Human Immunodeficiency Virus. It is the virus that causes AIDS. People can look and feel healthy and still have the HIV virus and can infect other people with it. HIV comes from a germ and can develop into AIDS.

What is AIDS?

AIDS means Acquired Immunodeficiency Syndrome. People with AIDS can get very sick and even die because their bodies can no longer defend themselves against the infection. Researchers are searching for new ways to help people feel better with AIDS or not get it at all.

Will I get AIDS?

A person can't get HIV from hugging or kissing someone, swimming with someone, or being near someone with a cough or sneeze. They can get HIV from sexual intercourse with another person who has HIV – like other sexually transmitted diseases. That is why practicing safe sex is important.

Can I get pregnant if I only have sex one time?

Yes, you can get pregnant with just one sexual experience. Anytime anyone has sexual intercourse there is the possibility of pregnancy. Using a condom or taking birth control medications are forms of contraceptives that can help prevent pregnancy. But the safest way not to get pregnant is to not have sex at all. This is called abstinence.

My friends say it's not a big deal to have sex. I'm only 11 and it seems scary. Are they right?

You don't have to have sex until you feel ready. I think your friends are wrong. Sex is an important part of life that should come with maturity. It is a good idea for teenagers to not have sex. Having sex can lead to teenage pregnancy or feelings of regret for doing something you weren't quite ready to do, or even a sexually transmitted disease. There are many other ways to show affection and caring for someone you like.

My friend Michelle says she has oral sex. What is oral sex?

It is an important question and I want to give you a thoughtful answer. Let me think about it. I was wondering what you heard about oral sex.

I'm not sure. Maybe it's – you know. When you talk about it. Is that right?

No, oral sex is another way of sexual expression. It is a form of stimulating another person's private parts using your mouth. Oral sex is a sexual activity and, like sexual intercourse, can lead to sexually transmitted infections.

That sounds gross. Yuck.

I know some things about sex might sound silly or ridiculous. It might make me giggle too. But you might change your mind in time. Sex will probably be a natural part of your life. Your questions are good and I am always happy to hear them.

Concluding thoughts

Children's natural curiosity about sex is sharpened through much of the media's grossly exaggerated distortions of sexuality and children. PG rated movies would have been rated as strictly adult viewing in past generations. They are now commonplace viewing on TV for today's children. Young people begin to model and act out what they see and hear without having the maturity or social sophistication to hold sexiness and its inferred behaviors at such a young age.

Advertising with young girls wearing tight skirts or using makeup can be branded as extreme and possibly inappropriate during family TV time. Pre-teens are influenced to look and act like teens or adults. Children are exposed to a false sexuality as they hear words and see images that don't match their limited life experience.

Growing up too fast and too soon without real understanding can be dangerous. Initiating conversations through referring to a pregnant woman, a special book, a new baby, or a kiss in a movie can open the door to entering a child's world and their perspective on issues involving sex. Young people pick up signals about sex and sexuality. Adults can transform suggestive messages and advertising into real information that can be trusted and helpful in making good choices.

Be prepared to give children and young teens accurate and age-appropriate information on normal child development. Be wary of media input. Be steadfast in labeling misinformation that may lead to inappropriate understandings and actions.

CHAPTER 6

What does puberty mean? Is my body going to change?

Sexuality has become commercialized and rebranded for younger and younger children, with a new target group for media marketing with young school students. Pre-adolescents represent a huge source of revenue. Girls and boys are just beginning to figure out who they are and want desperately to fit in with their peer group. Popularity is all too often equated with sexuality, with too many young children being bombarded by a media with suggestive sexuality and media-hyped self-serving monetary interests.

By the age of ten, many of these youngsters buy into the need to be sexy and sensual to have friends. Adults must be focused with laser accuracy on marketing manipulations in order to override unhealthy messages packaged in inappropriate commercialism. Coupled with media gross misrepresentations about sex is peer pressure and peer misinformation.

As they mature, children can become scared and worried when they hear from friends or see in the media ways their bodies may develop. It is important to prepare them ahead of time about the sudden changes their bodies will go through as they reach puberty. Even young school children can be told about puberty or bodily changes before they occur, helping to reduce future anxiety. With accurate information instead of unhealthy propaganda, children can understand their ever-changing bodies in a clear and safe way.

Tara (11): a case study

Tara walked in the door and blurted out "Mom, one of the girls at school had some blood on her pants and the kids made fun of her. What do I do if it happens to me?" She barely had a chance to put her backpack down and get a drink before Mom responded. "Pull up a chair. We need to talk." In the fastest voice Tara had ever heard, Mom scurried through a conversation at lightning speed. "If you ever have blood between your legs it means you are menstruating. It's called having your period. Then you can have a baby. It's when the lining of your uterus..."

Tara interrupted her mom in mid-sentence. "Mom! I know what it is. My teacher told us at school and Laura explained everything when it happened to her. I just want to know what to do!"

Mom looked down to the ground. "Sorry, it's just my mom never told me anything about menstruation and puberty, so I wanted to be sure you knew what it was." She then gave a more practical explanation. "I started menstruating at 12. You might take after me and start around then too. If you start to bleed at school you can go to the nurse or carry a pad in your purse. The pad fits in your underpants and absorbs the bleeding so it won't get on your clothes. That way you will be prepared and pro-tected."

Tara breathed a sigh of relief. "Thanks, Mom. That's a great idea."

What is puberty?

Puberty is a time when there are great physical changes and growth in girls' and boys' bodies. There are also new and powerful thoughts, feelings, and ideas as well. It is the time when you begin changing from a child into a grown-up.

Puberty can begin as early as eight and keep going through being a teenager. Often the onset of puberty begins with menstruation. It wasn't too long ago that moms and dads couldn't find the words to use to talk about this important step towards puberty. Now grown-ups are more comfortable talking about puberty and in some cultures even honor it as a right of passage from childhood to adulthood. They might have a cele-bration or ceremony or perform a ritual.

Is my body going to change?

Yes. Hormones are chemicals manufactured in different places in your body that cause the great changes. Certain hormones from your brain send a message to your ovaries to start producing sex hormones to cause the ovaries to produce an egg. An egg is a female sex cell. A boy's brain sends a message to his testicles to make sperm. This is the time children can get pregnant and have babies.

What is menstruation?

Menstruation is a part of a girl's growing up that usually last three to eight days. Blood may flow out of her vagina during this time and it will usually happen every month.

What causes menstruation?

During puberty the ovaries begin releasing an adult egg each month and this is called ovulation. The egg travels down the fallopian tube into the uterus. This is where the egg can join a sperm and develop into a baby. That means the egg is fertilized and the baby starts growing.

Can I fertilize an egg to make a baby grow in me?

This can only happen if you have sexual intercourse. Without having sexual intercourse the egg is not fertilized. It breaks down in the uterus along with blood and fluid in the uterus lining. The uterus lining begins to dissolve and passes out of the uterus through the vagina and out of the body. This dissolving occurs every month and is called menstruation.

Molly called menstruation getting your period. Is that right?

Yes. Getting your period is another way to say menstruation. It is a natural part of getting older. The first time a girl gets her period she may get scared or worried. That's why it helps to know about it ahead of time.

Sarah (9)

My big sister says my body is going to change as I grow up. That's scary. Why does my body have to change so much?

Your body has certain chemicals called hormones that signal growth as a boy or girl. Your hormones as a girl have created a vulva and vagina and as your body grows it will develop breasts, rounder hips, and pubic hair. Boy's hormones develop a larger penis and testicles, and as they get older hormones cause their voice to get lower and hair to grow in different parts of their body. It is nature's way of growing up.

How will I know I am going to menstruate?

That's a good question and it will help you to be prepared. About a year before you begin to menstruate you will begin to see hair grow around your pubic area and under your arms. This is a signal menstruation will be coming. Some girls can begin as early as 10 or 11, some not until their middle teens. Everyone's body works on their own unique clock.

What are signs to look for in puberty?
Both girls and boys sweat more and have more oily skin and hair. Both sexes grow a lot and gain weight. They both grow hair under their arms and around their private parts. But girls have changes that boys don't.

Their ovaries, breasts, and even their hips grow larger. A white fluid may come out of their vagina. Girls begin to menstruate in puberty. That's a lot of changes to watch for.

Mark (12)

I like knowing what happens to my sister's body during puberty. Do I go through changes during puberty too?
Yes, you do. Boys go through many changes too. During puberty the brain signals the testicles to produce a hormone called testosterone. Testosterone makes the body grow and produces millions of sperm, the male sex cells. A boy's scrotum keeps the sperm at just the right temperature to grow. Then they can travel out through the penis. The sperm mixes with fluid to create semen. When a man and woman have sex the sperm in the semen can fertilize the woman's egg and then the woman becomes pregnant and can have a baby.

What is semen?

Semen is a mixture of sperm and fluid that is white and sticky. This semen is often ejected from the penis. This is called ejaculation when the semen suddenly comes out. This ejaculation only happens when the penis is erect. It is called an erection when the muscles tighten in the penis. This usually lasts a few minutes and then the muscles relax. This can feel pleasurable or exciting. It is a real sign of puberty for a boy.

Sometimes semen comes out when I don't expect it to. Is that OK?

Yes, it is OK. It might come out when you are thinking about somebody you have a crush on, or someone in a bathing suit, or at night when you are asleep. You might have dreams about something sexual or someone you are thinking of. All of this is normal. If semen comes out while you are dreaming some grown-ups might call this a "wet dream."

What else will happen to my body when I reach puberty?

Your arms and legs will become longer and larger and you will probably gain weight and grow taller. Your muscles, your testicles, and your penis grow larger too. Your hair and skin may get oily and you may sweat more.

The hair on your head gets thicker and you grow hair on your chest, your face, under your arms, and around your penis.

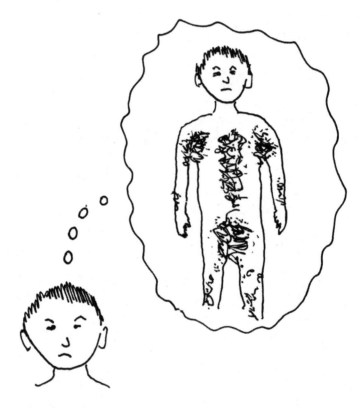

Concluding thoughts

There is a huge generational gap in comfort regarding discussing this subject. Many grandparents could not access the words to use. Today's children seem to know too much too soon and often share their knowledge with surprising if not shocking ease. The more children can talk to their parents about sexual issues and the more carefully they are listened to, the less likely they are to act out inappropriately as they grow older. Although it is natural to feel uncomfortable talking with children about sex, it is essential to explore uncomfortable feelings in order to feel confident when discussing the subject. It's OK to be honest too. Let them know you might feel uncomfortable because your parents were unable to speak about this subject. Be direct in saying you want an open conversation, and if you don't have all the answers, you are willing to find them out.

Use every moment as a teachable moment. There really is little or no embarrassment when these discussions are initiated before the child begins to get close to puberty. After puberty it is more difficult to have these conversations unless a foundation of honest and open dialog has already been created.

CHAPTER 7

Am I falling in love? How can I tell if it's love or just friends?

Children need to know that sexual relationships involve caring, intimacy, and affection in the same way they need to know definitions and biological facts about sex. It is essential that adults include a discussion with youngsters about sexual relationships and becoming responsible within that relationship. Adults can communicate their value system to children about sex, creating a core understanding as children struggle with the many issues involving sex as they mature.

Girls and boys will be better able to resist peer pressure and make good decisions if they have discussed issues involving the responsibilities and consequences of sexual activity with someone they trust. Even pre-teens can benefit from a discussion about unwanted pregnancy and ways to protect themselves against sexually transmitted diseases.

Susan (10): a case study

Susan and Robby are in the same mathematics class. They sit next to each other. Every time Susan thinks about mathematics she gets excited. She looks forward to being with Robby. Sometimes she thinks about him in English class too and imagines talking and laughing with him. She daydreams about what he says to her and that he even holds her hand. Her mom says she has a crush on Robby because she thinks about him and is so happy to see him.

Susan wonders if Robby feels the same way. What does it mean? How long will these feelings last?

What is a crush?

A crush is a feeling of liking someone and being attracted to them. This special person occupies your thoughts and feelings and creates a strong desire to be with them. Crushes are the beginning of having romantic feelings for someone.

How long does a crush last?

Crushes can last a long time, a few weeks, or a day. But no matter how long, these feelings are real and important.

Can I have a crush on someone of the same sex as me?

Yes. Sometime girls love a favorite movie star or boys really admire their coach and still have crushes on children their age of the same or opposite sex. When young people are attracted romantically to the opposite sex as they grow up, it is called being straight or heterosexual. If they are attracted romantically to the same sex it is called gay or homosexual.

What is falling in love?

Falling in love is being attracted romantically to another person and really liking who they are. People in love like to be together in many ways. They may hug and kiss, take walks and talk, or play sports together. They begin to feel they would like to spend life together and plan a future that can include marriage and family.

What can I do if I like Robby a lot?

Keep liking him. Get to know him. Go to parties, talk and laugh with him, and see how that feels. You might want to go to the movies or bowling with Robby and a group of other friends. See what you have in common and if you like the same things. Your crush may last for just a little while or it may grow. When you are old enough and you have these feelings you can begin to date someone like Robby by going out with him for dinner or a movie, or to a ball game. For now it would be fun to spend time with Robby at a party or school dance or just talking.

Alex (11)

I watch TV and see people kiss. In the next scene they are having a baby. Do people have sex as soon as they meet?

TV and movies often show people meeting and having sex right away. And you are right – lots of times you see a kiss and then a pregnant mom. But in real life dating can be a sweet and important time to be with someone you like and to get to know him or her.

What does dating really mean?

Dating is when you like someone very much and want to be with him or her and get to know him or her. Usually children start dating in their middle teens if they want to. They don't have to. It may involve some sexual activity, like kissing and hugging, but it can also include feelings of deep friendship. Dating can be lots of fun at the right time, but for children your age you can get experience with being attracted to someone by being in groups with other boys and girls. You will feel more ready to date when you get older.

What do people do on dates?

They take time to get to know each other. They might go to the movies together, play sports, eat ice cream, have a picnic, or just hang out together and talk. The more time they spend with each other, the more they decide if they want to continue to date because they just like being together and are attracted to each other. And it doesn't mean you have to have sex. Dating is not equal to sex.

What does it mean to be attracted to each other?

It means you think of that other person in a caring way. You like them, you have romantic or sexual feelings towards them, and you get a feeling of closeness in communicating and sharing your minds and hearts about life in lots of ways. And you might miss the person a lot when you are alone.

Concluding thoughts

As children mature they begin to wonder about new feelings they have of attraction to friends and peers. Sometimes adults tell them they have a crush on someone, and may minimize or tease them about these tender feelings. This may not only constrict the flow of dialogue but may also cause a young person to feel ashamed about honest feelings.

Girls and boys also wonder about falling in love, and how to distinguish between a crush, friendship, attraction, and love. They ask about sexual activity and intimacy and seek ways to learn to navigate the currents involved with sexuality and love. Reminding them there is no rush to growing up too fast or dating too soon is important. It allows them safety with age-appropriate feelings and behaviors and the ability to withstand peer pressure and society's over-sexualizing of young people.

CHAPTER 8

What is gender?
Do girls and boys
have to act and feel
a certain way?

An essential idea for children to incorporate throughout their growing up is that girls and boys don't have to act, dress, or talk a certain way because they are born a girl or boy. Gender is the sex one is born with as male or female. We don't need to label things as "girl colors and boy colors," "girl games and boy games" or "girl toys or boy toys" determined by gender.

Children are different from one another and unique. They can choose their own path of what to say, do, or look like that feels right just for them, regardless of their gender. Adults can model dialogues that are free of gender stereotyping and encourage children to partici-pate in a wide variety of play with different kinds of toys and games. They can support the caring and creative side of boys and the leadership qualities and physical strength of girls. This helps both sexes to express them-selves more freely. Suggesting children play with toys, pick a sport, or choose their clothing according to interest, comfort, and personal taste is important.

Ben (7): a case study

Ben was having a difficult time in second grade. One day he came home from school crying. "They keep teasing me at school. I can't take it anymore." "Calm down, Ben," Mom said, "and tell me what happened." "Joey and Mike keep calling me names. They say you're so weird all day long. And why don't you cut your hair – you look like a girl. I hate them! I'm never going back to school."

Ben slammed the door and wouldn't come out for dinner. The next morning, to everyone's surprise, at the breakfast table they saw Ben had cut his hair. And it was short.

He thought the teasing would stop, but it didn't. Joey and Mike just chided him when they saw him. "Now your hair is too short. You still look weird to me."

I liked having long hair but was so tired of being teased. Why do children make fun of boys with long hair?

It is called gender stereotyping. That means children have rules about how girls should look and how boys should look and how they should act and even what they should wear.

What does gender mean?

Gender means what sex you are. It means whether you are a boy or a girl.

Sometimes parents, teachers, friends, relatives, and even TV put a lot of pressure on girls and boys to fit into expectations of what they should be or do. But you should be able to have hair any way you like. It is your hair. You don't have to be a certain gender, girl or boy, to look and dress the way that feels right for you.

But children teased me so much about my hair, I just cut it all off. And they still called me names. Why?

I can't really say why these children are still teasing you, but sometimes children just like to be mean or think they are funny. Sometimes they say things and don't even understand what they are saying. And sometimes, if they know it is upsetting they may continue to make fun of something. Now that you know they might tease you again, you can be prepared and practice for the next time.

What can I practice to do and say?

"I am a boy. I am myself. I like my hair just the way it is." Then you can laugh about it or just walk away. There is nothing more to say. Can you practice that with me?

Yes I can. I want them to stop teasing. How can I make them stop?

That is a good question. Find children to be with who aren't mean and don't tease. Stay with them. Have a friend with you if you think you will be around a person you know is mean. Practice what to do and say when someone teases you. Children who tease are called bullies.

What is a bully?

A bully is someone who uses his or her power to be mean and hurt other people. They can be tall or short, older or younger, a girl or a boy. Bullies come in all shapes and sizes. Teasing and making fun of someone for how they look, dress, or what they like to do is called bullying. Lots of bullies like children to get upset. It might help not to show it if you are.

But what if the bullies don't stop?

Talk to adults about the bullying and teasing. If one doesn't offer to help, find another one to talk with. You can talk to parents, teachers, school counselors or nurses, or even the principal or a police officer.

If you see someone else is being bullied, don't be afraid to tell someone. That is helping them. Some children even leave a note about bullying with their teacher and don't sign their name. That way they won't have to worry about the bully hurting them.

Wouldn't I just be a snitch or tattletale if I tell on someone?

No, definitely not! Telling and tattling are two different things. Snitching or tattling is talking about children to get them into trouble. Telling is helping children out of trouble. It is important to tell and get help if someone is hurting you or someone else.

What can I do to have children like me just the way I am?

To be liked and accepted for who you are, you need to accept and respect yourself.

What does it mean to be accepted?

Being accepted means being liked for being ourselves just the way we are. We shouldn't feel pressure to change or feel judged. Girls and boys can be who they are and do what feels right for them and feel confident and strong inside, which is perfectly all right. That's how it should be.

Mia (9)

Joey and Sam say I'm a girl and can't play games with them. Is that fair?

It is not fair to exclude people because they are a girl or a boy. It makes them feel bad and left out. Girls and boys can play together and have lots of fun.

Tommy likes to play with stuffed animals and Joey says he is acting like a girl. Is that true?

No, that is not true. He is playing with what he likes. That's all. Sometimes girls like to play with action figures even though people might say that's a boy thing to do. Lots of children like to play with stuffed animals and action figures.

Pete (5)

I like pink and I'm a boy. Nellie says only girls can wear pink. Can I be a boy and wear pink?

Of course you can. Some people want you to think there are only some colors for girls and some for boys. They say pink is for girls and blue is for boys. But children like all kinds of colors, and they should be able to choose whatever colors they like best.

I'm a real boy and I can wear pink. Right?

Right. And I am a girl and love blue. We don't have to listen when TV or other people say we have to wear something because of our gender. Wear what feels good to you. That is the right thing to do.

I like to paint and bake cookies. Is that a girl thing to do?

It can be a girl thing and a boy thing. Painting and baking cookies are activities all children can enjoy. Boys and girls can like both and that is OK. We don't need to label things as "girl colors and boy colors," "girl games and boy games" or "girl toys and boy toys." Many of the world's most famous artists and chefs are men. And some of the best athletes have been women.

Everyone is different and unique. It is important not to just say "boys can only do this" and "girls can do that," but that "children can do lots of things."

But Patrick calls me a sissy and a wimp. What do they mean?

Sissy is a word children may call a boy if they think he is doing what some people think is a girl thing, like sewing or cooking. But tailors and top fashion designers are often men.

Wimp is a word for calling someone weak or saying they don't have courage. Sometimes children call a boy a wimp if he cries or doesn't play sports.

I cry and don't play sports. but I can jump off of a diving board. Am I still brave?

Yes, you are. Boys can be brave for diving off a board and girls can be brave for climbing a tree. Sometimes girls and boys can show courage just for coming to school with a new haircut, or wearing glasses for the first time. Being a girl or boy doesn't make you brave, but how you act and what you do does!

Amy (10)

Kate called me a tomboy because I love to play football. What is a tomboy?

Sometimes people will call a girl a tomboy if she likes only to do what people think of as boy things, like climbing trees, playing sports, and wearing jeans instead of dresses. Girls can play football and wear dresses too. They have lots of choices. Try reading *Just like Josh Gibson* by Angela Johnson (see Appendix 3: Useful websites and resources). It's about a little girl who loved baseball and wanted to be on the team, but wasn't allowed, because at that time it was only a boys' sport. Her determination won and she was eventually made the first girl on the boy's baseball team.

That sounds like a good story. But what about now? Can girls play in all sports?

Yes, they can. There are teams for girls in soccer, basketball and baseball. Girls have become very valued sports figures who are respected for their accomplishments. Now girls and boys can play many games together without thinking it is just for a girl or boy. Then no one feels left out.

I hate wearing dresses. People say I should dress like a girl. What does that mean?

That means they have an idea in their heads about how girls should dress. You don't have to listen. Clothing should feel good and be a way of expressing yourself. You can dress for comfort and wear what you like. Girls can like and wear trousers and dresses and skirts and shirts. You are still a girl, whatever you wear.

Brigette (6)

My mom and dad gave me a baby carriage and I turned it into a wagon for my cars and trucks. Dad got angry and made me put it back. He said girls play with dolls, not trucks. I don't like dolls. What is wrong with making a wagon?

Nothing. That was a very creative and fun idea. Then you can choose to make your toy a carriage for dolls or a wagon for cars and trucks. It's nice for children to have choices with toys, and pick the ones that feel right to play with. Some people think girls have to play with what they think is "girl stuff," like dolls and pink crayons, and boys have to play with they think is "boy stuff," like action figures. Children can like all types of toys. Picking toys that are the most fun for you is the best way to choose.

Concluding thoughts

As caring adults we can provide responses for children to practice in response to sexual stereotyping. Adults can model a dialogue free of gender bias that includes jobs, toys, clothing, and colors. They can create gender-neutral conversations, eliminating phrases like "girls do this" and "boys do that" and present broader statements such as "children can play this game" or "children can wear lots of colors." In this way young people are supported in expressing themselves freely without being confined to limited societal restraints. This can be achieved by encouraging boys in their sensitivity and creative pursuits and girls with their sports abilities and strength. All children can be encouraged to participate in a wide variety of play containing many choices in toys, sports, and other activities based on interest and not gender.

It is important to define bullying for children as when someone is mean in a physical way or hurts their feelings – stressing this is unacceptable and maintaining strong guidelines against it. Providing words to explain expressions such as tomboy and wimp allows girls and boys to discuss their meaning and present gender-neutral understandings. We can educate young children with the idea that everyone is unique and each person has their own likes and dislikes. This concept can help erode gender bias and empower children to be just who they are and do what comes naturally to them with freedom and acceptance.

CHAPTER 9

What does gay mean? What does straight mean?

Young children are very inquisitive. Many questions center on girl and boy topics. Answering children's questions about gender issues has become a prime focus for caring adults in the twenty-first century. As parents, educators, or helping professionals we must be aware of words to use when answering questions about being gay or straight. Too often misinformation on these subjects can result in gender stereotyping, sometimes leading to low self-esteem, internalization of teasing, and depression for children from a young age to adolescence. Creating a clear and nonjudgmental language for dialogue is an essential step in the elimination of this prejudice.

As children get older they may wonder what words such as wimp, tomboy, sissy, and gay really mean. They often hear these words said in school to tease and make fun of others. It is important to use clearly defined terms and underscore to children that these words are hurtful. They need to be given accurate information.

Young people are naturally curious about sexual orientation and gender identity and are inundated with information and images on this subject through film and TV and older peers. Real definitions for gay, lesbian, bisexual, and transgender people are helpful in distinguishing myths and gender bias from facts. We can begin by creating the paradigm with children that we live in a gay and straight world.

Mia (11): a case study

Mia loves her Uncle Ryan very much. He is kind and caring and always fun to be with. He loves to take her bike riding in the park and buy her an ice cream. Uncle Ryan lives with another man, his partner Anthony. Mia wonders if they are a couple because they seem to love each other. They live together and hold hands and hug each other a lot. One day Mia heard Uncle Ryan say to Mom, "One day I would like to get married to Anthony and be a family and have children." "How can that be?" Mia wondered. "How can two men get married and have children?"

Mom explained to Mia that Ryan and Anthony are gay. She explained another word for gay is homosexual. Mia wondered again.

What does gay or homosexual mean?

Homosexuality is a word for people who are attracted romantically, physically, and emotionally to people of the same sex. Sometimes people use the word gay to mean the same thing as homosexual.

Gay can mean a man can like another man or a woman can like another woman the way that a mom and dad like each other. Uncle Ryan and Anthony are gay. They are two men who are attracted in a loving way to each other and want to be in a loving relationship with each other.

Sometimes children at school make fun of gay people. Why?

Maybe they have heard bad information from other people or seen negative things on TV, or maybe they are just afraid of people who are different. But no one should make fun of other people for being who they are.

If Uncle Ryan and Anthony are homosexual or gay, what are you?

I am a woman who is in a loving relationship with a man I am attracted to physically and emotionally. I am a heterosexual.

My friend Elizabeth said her parents are straight. What does that mean?

Some people use the word straight as another word for heterosexual. You could say your mom and dad are straight. That means they have a sexual and loving attraction to someone of the opposite sex.

Is it wrong to be gay?

No, it is not wrong. Most gay people say they don't have a choice. They feel they were born gay just the same as straight people are born straight. Being gay is not a sickness. Even psychiatrists, doctors who help people with their thoughts and feelings, agree that being gay is not a sickness. Being gay or straight is just the way people express their romantic and sexual love.

Somebody at school said people could be sexually attracted to both sexes. Is that true?

Yes, it is true. It is called being bisexual. That means a person who is attracted sexually and romantically to both men and women.

Can Uncle Ryan and Anthony get married?

In some places. A small number of countries in the world have passed laws allowing same-sex couples to marry. Some countries have laws against same-sex marriage and these laws are just beginning to change. Lots of times people have been afraid to make laws for same-sex marriage because it seems too different to them. However, in many places, legal arrangements for same-sex couples called civil unions or domestic partnerships are allowed. Same-sex couples sometimes have their own religious or private commitment ceremonies if legal marriages are not yet passed where they live.

Legalizing same-sex marriage is sometimes called marriage equality. Marriage equality would give same-sex couples the same rights and privileges that the rest of the citizens in their countries have. Sometimes they can't take care of each other in the hospital and sometimes they have to pay a lot more money in taxes or can't get insurance.

Can gay people have children?

Yes, gay people can have children and many do. They can adopt a child. Same-sex women couples can choose a procedure called alternative or artificial insemination, a way to get pregnant and have a baby. Sometimes gay people live a straight life and have children with an opposite sex partner. Then they realize they are really gay, but they remain caring parents for their children.

Experts say gay parents make just as good moms and dads as straight parents. You can read about a family with two dads that have lots of adventures with pets in the book *A Pet of My Own* by Ursula Ferro (see Appendix 3: Useful websites and resources). It shows gay parents can and do create loving families.

Suzie (10)

Meg called the gym teacher a "lesbo." Mary said her moms are lesbians and she started to cry. What does lesbian mean?

A lesbian is a woman who likes another woman the way moms and dads like each other. They want to be with each other and share life together, and they feel a romantic and sexual attraction for each other. Sometimes they want to get married and raise children the same way that straight couples do.

I like Mary a lot. Does that mean I'm a lesbian?

No, it doesn't mean you are a lesbian. Girls also really like their girlfriends and boys really like their boyfriends at your age. It can get confusing. As you grow up and become a teenager, you will naturally understand which gender you are really attracted to sexually and romantically.

Jon (9)

I saw a show on TV about transgender people. I wasn't sure what that meant. What is transgender?

We can think of a transgender person as someone who is born a girl but has a boy's brain or someone who is born a boy but really has a girl's brain inside. Because they have brains that work like their opposite biological sex they may have a boy's body but think and feel like a girl or a girl's body but think and feel like a boy.

That must be hard for them. Do they get teased?

Yes, Jon, they do get teased for seeming different. It is hard for gay, lesbian, bisexual, and transgender people. Some girls and boys may think they are bad or wrong for being *who* they are. Then they begin to feel bad when they are called names or teased in other ways. Children can be afraid of what they don't understand. The more we get to know people we think are different, the more we can learn they are really a lot like us. Everyone is unique and different in his or her own way.

Mathew (6)

I'm a boy, but I like to play with stuffed animals... Jack said "You're so gay." What did he mean?

I'm not sure. Jack might not even know gay really means two men or two women who like each other the way moms and dads do. Sometimes children hear the words "that's so gay" so much they say it without even thinking about it. Children may explain, "I'm just kidding" or "it's just a joke" and think "you're so gay" is a fun thing to say. But if it hurts you it is not really funny. When it sounds like it is making fun or teasing someone about being different, then it is not OK.

If I like Max, does that mean I'm gay?

No, that just means you like your friend Max. It is fine and natural to like boys and girls at your age. When you get older and begin to have more grown-up relationships you will know which person you like in a romantic or loving way instead of the way you like Max just as a good friend right now.

Melissa (8)

Doris has two gay dads, does that mean all of her grandparents are gay too? Will she grow up gay too?

No, it doesn't. Moms and dads don't raise their children to be gay or straight. They raise their children to grow up naturally and realize their own sexual orientation or gender identity. Just because your dad is gay doesn't mean his mom and dad are gay. Just because a dad is gay doesn't mean his child is gay. You can't catch being gay or get it the way you inherit blue eyes from your father. Most gay and straight people say they didn't choose their feelings of attraction to the same or opposite sex. It was always a part of them.

Concluding thoughts

Adults can help shift outdated thought forms containing gender bias into an expanded vision of acceptability and respect for everyone, regardless of gender issues. Giving children accurate definitions involving sexual orientation and gender identity helps create acceptance of all people and eliminate bias, while helping to minimize fears and self-consciousness.

Children are bombarded with images of the perfect male or female, and they begin trying in pre-school to live up to an unrealistic and impossible stereotype for their gender. Dispelling cultural myths about gender attributes and qualities can increase the sense of freedom for children as they grow up to be who they are rather than who others think they should be. Showing respect and inclusion for gay and straight people in conversation and action sets the tone for an inclusive and safe environment for all children.

CHAPTER 10

Are there different kinds of families? What makes a family?

Talking with children about sex, pregnancy, birth, and babies leads to a natural discussion about families. Although the "average family" may still consist of a mom and dad and brothers and sisters living together, in today's world this is far from necessarily the case. Economic or social life situations can create a need for grandparents to raise their children's children. Other families include a single parent, perhaps through the death or abandonment of one parent. Some families are multicultural and diverse.

Children need to know that some parents are not able to have babies naturally through sexual intercourse because their egg and sperm cannot join together. There are other ways to have a baby. That is why some mothers and fathers adopt or have artificial insemination. Girls and boys who are adopted are a part of a real family that has a mom and dad. Children with same-sex parents can have two moms or two dads.

Creating teachable moments during family TV time or through a display of photographs at school with all kinds of babies, children, mothers, and fathers can begin to anchor the core concept that just as everyone is unique, every family is unique too. Families come in lots of shapes, sizes, and relationships. The underlying principle is that loving and taking care of each other is what really makes a family.

Harvey (7): a case study

Harvey spent much of his time looking in the mirror. He wished he didn't look so different from everyone else in the family. He studied the family picture on the piano with great concern and thoughtfulness. "Mom," Harvey explained over and over again, "I wish I looked like you and Dad and my sister Lizzie. I wish I had your blue eyes, and Dad's big smile. I wish I had Lizzie's beautiful hair. My friend Adam said Lizzie couldn't be my sister because she doesn't look like me. He said brothers and sisters look alike and that you and Dad can't be my real family because we don't look alike either. I tried to tell Adam that Lizzie and I are adopted, but he kept saying families should look alike. Are we still a family if I am adopted?"

Are we still a family if I am adopted?

Yes, you can be adopted and be part of a family. Parents don't just give birth to babies – they can adopt them too. Girls and boys and moms and dads sometimes look alike and sometimes look different. You and Lizzie look different from each other and your parents because you came from South America and Lizzie came from China. Your mom and dad wanted you very much and decided to adopt you from other countries. They brought you home when you were babies. They took pictures of your countries and made a special album for each of you. Your mom and dad loved and cared for you and Lizzie.

Well then... what makes us a family?

You are a family because you are girls and boys and moms and dads who love and care for each other. Some families like yours have children who are adopted and can have many cultures and races. Girls and boys can have families with a mom and dad, only one dad or one mom, two moms or two dads, or a grandmother and her grandchild. You might be the only child in your family. Your best friend could have a brother and sister. There are lots of ways to be a family. They come in all sizes and have different people in them. The important part of a family is shared respect and love.

I know what love is, but what does respect mean?

Respect is a word that means we accept other people without judging them. Girls and boys can be who they are and do what feels right to them and live in many special kinds of families. Being respectful is accepting people and their families just for who they are.

Steve says he was adopted too. He has a birth mother and his mom and dad. What does that mean?

Sometimes moms and dads can't have a baby and they decide to adopt one. They bring the baby into their family and are their legal parents. This baby is offered for adoption by his or her biological or birth mother. Some girls and boys meet their birth mother and some don't. There can be many reasons why a birth mother would feel someone else should have her baby. She may have been too young to raise a child or just not able to care for her children. She may have been very sick or may have died. Birth mothers can be from the same country as adoptive parents or from a far away country. Many children around the world get adopted just like Steve.

So – who is Steve's real mom?

Steve's real mom is the mother who takes care of him. His mom and dad adopted him for his entire life. Steve might not look a lot like his mom and dad, but they are his family. His biological mother that gave birth to him is called his birth mother.

Alan (11)

Nicole's mom has light skin and her dad has dark skin. Nicole's skin is in the middle. Can it still be a family if everyone has different color skin?

Of course it can. Babies, children, moms and dads can look alike or different. Some girls and boys may look like their moms or dads and others don't look like anyone in their family. The people in your family don't have to look like each other. Every family has its own special appearance, and no two families really look the same. What makes families the same is the love, caring, and respect everyone feels for each other. Nicole is a biological mixture of the races of her biological mom and dad.

How can people in the same family have different skin colors?

If people have different skin colors, we can say they may be a different race. Nicole's mom is white and her dad is African-American. Nicole is a mixture of African-American and white. They are still a family even though they are a different race. They are a multiracial family and can share their own unique backgrounds and cultures with each other.

Carlos's mom is from Mexico and his dad is from the United States. They look different and sound different too. Can they still be a family?

Yes again. Moms and dads can come from different cultures and have babies and children from different cultures. Children and parents can be born and grow up in different countries. They may not sound alike, practice the same customs, or even look alike. But they are alike in a lot of ways. They like to cook together and sing songs. Their cultures might be different but what is important is that they belong to each other, take care of each other, and love each other. They are a multicultural family.

Rosemary (6)

Janie says I don't have a real family. She says two dogs can be in a family but not two moms. But I have two moms. Is it true that two moms and a child aren't a real family?

No, that is not true. Families come in all different sizes, structures, and relationships.

You have two moms, two dogs and you, and that is your family. Families are babies, children, moms and dads that love and care for each other. Pets are parts of families too.

More people are beginning to understand that a family can have two moms or two dads. Sometimes people don't understand what they are not used to seeing. The more same-sex parents and their girls and boys let other people get to know them, the more familiar they become and the more they will be accepted. Other people will learn what you already know – you and your moms are a family because you love and care for each other.

Sometimes children ask me who my real mom is. What do I say?

That is hard because *you know* both of your moms are your real moms. And that is what you can say. Both my moms are real. Sometimes children with same-sex parents feel better if they have two moms or two dads who are their legal parents equally. That would help make it fair. Then children of same-sex parents would have the same benefits or rights under the law as other children do. Now they don't in lots of places.

Dennis (8)

Rosemary has two moms, but I have a mom and dad. Can there really be different kinds of families?

Absolutely. Girls and boys can live with their aunts and uncles, their grandparents, moms and dads, two moms, two dads, just one parent, or an older brother or sister. They can be adopted and live with adoptive parents or foster care parents.

If you want to see how your family is alike and different compared to other families you can read the book *Families* by Susan Kuklin (see Appendix 3: Useful websites and resources). It has interesting photographs and stories about lots of babies, children, moms, dads, and grandparents too.

Alex lives with a foster care mom. Is that a family?

Alex's mom and dad died. There were no family members for him to live with. That is called being an orphan. The courts gave him a guardian or foster care home. Now he has a temporary mom and dad who care for and protect him – his foster care parents. That is his family for now. Foster care parents temporarily take the place of moms and dads.

Thomas and his brother Joseph live with Grandma Stella. Is that a family?

Yes, it is. Thomas's mom and dad died and Grandma Stella became his legal guardian. A guardian is not a real mom or dad but someone the courts appointed to take care of a girl or boy. Being a guardian means she isn't his real mom but she does take care of him like a mom. There was no one else to care for Thomas and Joseph after their mom and dad died. Children are called orphans if their parents die. Sometimes they have guardians if their moms or dads can't take care of them even if they are still living. Their moms and dads may be too sick or not have any money.

Grandma Stella is the guardian for Thomas and Joseph. She helps them with their homework, makes dinner, and gives them both lots of hugs and kisses. That is a family.

Nell (9)

I live with my mom and dad. I am the only child. How many people do there have to be to make a family?

Families can be big and small. Some families may have one baby and others can have loads of girls and boys. Some families are large, with lots of brothers and sisters, aunts and uncles, and grandparents. But your family is small. It is you, Dad and Mom. Your grandparents have died and you have an Aunt Joan and Uncle Burt and a cousin named Denise. That is your family, a girl with a mom and dad who love and care for each other.

Amelia's mom and dad are divorced. She lives with her mom most of the time, but when she visits her dad she has a little sister and a stepmom. Can Amelia have two families?

Absolutely. Sometimes moms and dads stay together and sometimes they separate and then get divorced. Divorced means parents are not married anymore. Boys and girls can have lots of grown-ups to support and care for them if that happens. When moms and dads separate or divorce, babies and older girls and boys often have two different homes to live in. Sometimes when a mom and dad remarry, the two families come together and create a bigger family. They can include having a step-parent, being a stepchild, or having new brothers and sisters as both families grow.

Trevor's dad got married again after Trevor's mom died. His stepmother had two children, Audrey and Patrick. Now they all live together in the same house. Is that a family?

Yes, it is. Moms and dads can remarry. Then two families come together to make a new one. Biological moms and dads, stepmothers and stepfathers, biological brothers and sisters, stepsiblings, and even cats and dogs from both families now are together. Moms and dads, stepmothers and stepfathers, babies, and older girls and boys can live together. This is called a blended family.

Aunt Helen and Uncle Jake don't have children – just Maggie and Felix, their dog and cat. Can you still have a family without children?

Yes, you can, Nell. Pets can also be part of a family. Aunt Helen and Uncle Jake say Maggie and Felix are like their children. They treat them like their "babies" because they love and care for them.

George just lives with his mom. Is that too little to be a family?

No – not at all. George and his mom are a single parent family. Lots of children live with just their mother or just their father. The other parent may have died, got very sick, or left for another reason and never came back. Families can be just one mom or one dad and one baby or child that love and care for each other. They can't be too big or too small.

Concluding thoughts

Most babies and older girls and boys grow up in families where they are loved and taken care of. Sometimes babies are born into families with a mom and dad, sometimes they are adopted and still have a mom and dad. Families are as rich and varied as the people who make them up. Families can have one baby or lots of boys and girls; they can have a mother and father, stepmothers and stepfathers, or only one mom and dad or two moms and two dads. Babies and boys and girls can live with grandparents, just one parent, guardians, and foster moms and dads too. Mothers and fathers and their children can be different races and cultures. Families are a kaleidoscope of the diversity that encompasses human beings and can be valued for their uniqueness and special qualities.

Imprinting for children at a young age that families are girls and boys and moms and dads, guardians, grandparents, and even pets who love and care for each other is important. Inclusiveness and understanding surrounding race, culture, gay and lesbian issues, adoption, foster care, divorce, and single parenting solidify acceptance of all families and acknowledge that differences are OK and natural in today's multifaceted world.

A final note

The childhood journey on the quest for information and understanding about sex is a long and patient interchange between young people and adults.

Answering children's questions about sex is a tender topic that begins the first time you hold your baby in your arms. Curiosity and awareness of touching and body parts are natural and healthy. As children grow, their questions about sex become spontaneous and important. Some answers may only be yes or no. Others may be more in depth, depending on the child's curiosity and age-appropriate satisfaction with the response. Girls' and boys' questions may begin with "why," and our answers can involve realistic facts and valued philosophy. Each adult has a unique style of explanation, and young children learn to anticipate this as they mature.

The often dreaded *sex talk* parents fear they will face as their children enter adolescence actually begins with the wonderment of a young child asking, "Where do babies come from?" By starting with simply explaining a baby is inside a big belly to sharing a more grown up definition of sexual intercourse we can build a strong and intimate bond with a child. This bond grows into mutual trust as the child matures. A shared respect nurtures honesty in families and schools rather than having young people relying on myths and misinformation from the media and peers. Pro-active adults can be pivotal in establishing a solid and realistic appreciation of the many joys, complexities, and human commonality we all share on the topic of sex.

A checklist for children

- Ask questions. Don't be afraid.
- Exploring your body is OK.
- Learn the accurate words for body parts.
- Find out the facts about sex.
- Say _no_ to any touching that doesn't feel right.
- Tell an adult about any touching you don't like.
- Check out information you hear. Don't believe everything you learn from TV, the computer, or friends.
- Remember all questions are acceptable.
- Find a comfortable person to talk with about sex.
- Be your own person. Don't give into peer pressure.
- Practice and prepare a response to teasing.
- Stand up against mean behavior.
- Learn the difference between telling and tattling or snitching.
- Telling is OK. It can help someone.
- Accept other children just the way they are. They can be, say, or do what they like as long as they don't hurt anyone.
- Look for different kinds of families. All families are special.

For caring adults

What can we do?

- Encourage communication. Children need to know they can talk to parents about anything.

- Initiate discussion. "Did you notice Aunt Ellen is going to have a baby. Her tummy is so big and the baby is inside. How do you think it got there?"

- Start early. Begin to teach in a soft way for the very young child. Include in a toddler's vocabulary "eyes," "nose," "penis," and "vagina" to ensure appropriate labeling of body parts.

- Maintain a safe environment. Build a nonjudgmental environment free of punishment or reprisal about discussing sex.

- Honor and respect children's questions. Remember they are a signal to what they are thinking and feeling.

- Understand children's questions and concerns. Check with your child about the facts of what you heard them ask and what they mean.

- Listen carefully to your child and respect your child's views.

- Remind young people that thoughts and feelings about sex are common.

- Remain calm. Children are often satisfied with clear, simple, and factual responses. Wait to see if more is needed.

- Say the correct words for genitals. Having a common and correct language helps children and adults navigate the world they live in.

- Practice your response to different questions about sex in order to feel confident when the discussion arises. The more comfortable you can be the more you create a positive and natural message about sex and gender issues for your child.

- Remember you don't need to know all the answers. It's OK to admit we don't have the answers and can invite children to join us in finding out together.

- Don't automatically assume misconduct. Children can ask questions about things without necessarily being experimental in real life.

- Be prepared with age-appropriate resources on sex and suggestions of other adults they may feel more comfortable with in discussing the topic of sex. Suggestions include pediatricians, teachers, guidance counselors or the school nurse.

- Explore your attitudes. Children who feel they can have open dialogue with their parents are less likely to later manifest high-risk behaviors. If you are fearful of the subject find material to learn from. Your confidence will grow as you explore the subject.

- Have a sense of humor. It creates a relaxed and open family environment.

- Work on overcoming anxiety related to discussing sex. Be open to questions.

- Answer questions as they come up. There is no one "birds and bees" talk.

- Beginning conversations with young children on sex lays the groundwork for a comfortable and continuous process as children grow and mature.

- Providing information is not equal to permission. A good combination of the message of abstinence, self-control, accurate information on birth control, and sexually transmitted diseases is helpful.

- We can't control whether or not our children have sex at an early age, but we don't have to automatically assume they will.

- Being flexible and understanding encourages a child's development of a healthy self-image, creating a stronger resistance to societal and peer pressure and reducing a child's natural tendency to rebel.

Useful websites and resources

Websites

United States

www.childrensgrief.net

Linda Goldman's website includes information on bullying, sexual stereotyping, and gender issues concerning children and teens.

www.SIECUS.org

SIECUS is a website for the Sexuality Information and Educational Council of the United States.

www.plannedparenthood.org

Planned Parenthood Federation of America, Inc. offers information on sex education, birth control, pregnancy, and sexually transmitted disease.

www.advocatesforyouth.org/parents/index.htm

Advocates for Youth provides a parents sex education center with information and guidelines.

www.parentstv.org

Parents' Television Council offers a parents guide, family guide, and rating system to promote parent responsibility for children's TV viewing.

www.familyeducation.com/home/

Network for Family Life Education presents information on bullying and growing up too fast.

www.teachingtolerance.org

The Teaching Tolerance website provides information on gender issues and sexual stereotyping for children and pre-teens.

www.glsen.org

GLSEN The Gay, Lesbian and Straight Education Network works with schools to educate and provide safety and respect for all students, regardless of sexual orientation or gender identity/expression.

www.colage.org

COLAGE Children of Lesbian and Gay Everywhere is an organization whose support and activism is by and for people with gay, lesbian, bisexual, and/or transgender parents and families.

www.pflag.org

PFLAG Parents, Families and Friends of Lesbians and Gays is an organization promoting the health and well-being of gay, lesbian, bisexual and transgender young people and adults, as well as their friends and families.

www.naeyc.org

National Association for the Education of Young Children is an organization dedicated to many topics related to gender issues and young children.

Great Britain

www.bbc.co.uk/science/humanbody/body/articles/lifecycle/teenagers/sexual_changes.shtml

This BBC website contains information on subjects such as puberty.

www.bbc.co.uk/science/humanbody/body/index.shtml?lifecycle

This site on the BBC website shows images of the male and female body.

www.ncb.org.uk

The National Children's Bureau shares a sexual health project to improve young people's access to sexual health services and sex and relationships education.

www.fpa.org.uk

The Family Planning Association is a sexual health charity whose purpose is to enable people to make informed choices about sex and enjoy sexual health.

www.respond.org.uk

UK organization providing advice on the issue of sexual abuse.

www.nas.org.uk/nas/jsp/polopoly.jsp?d=296&a=6001

> The National Autistic Society provides advice on sex education and children and young people with ASD.

Canada

www.ucalgary.ca/resolve/violenceprenention/English/reviewprog/youth dprogs.htm#pro17

> Making Waves is a Canadian organization working with relationship, boundaries and sexual abuse issues with younger and older teens.

www.cfsh.ca

> The Canadian Federation for Sexual Health presents ideas on how to create conversations about sex with your teen.

www.sexualityandu.ca

> The Society of Obstetricians and Gynecologists of Canada provides a resource for information on questioning the need to talk to children about sex.

www.canadianparents.com

> Canadian Parents: Canada's Parenting Community offers parents insights into dialoging with children about sex.

Australia

www.fpnsw.org.au

> Family Planning NSW provides trainings on sexual health and resources on sexual topics for children and teens.

www.raisingchildren.net.au

> Raising Children Network provides parents with tips for talking with children about sexuality.

www.kidspot.com.au

> Kidspot gives information on speaking with children about sex and keeping safe.

Resources for children

A Pet of My Own

by Ursula Ferro (2008, West Tisbury, MA: Marti Books). This is a story about Gabe and his two dads and their adventures with lots of animals (ages 5–11).

Families

by Susan Kuklin (2006, New York: Hyperion Books). Children from many different kinds of families talk about their diverse lives (ages 6–11).

Just Like Josh Gibson

by Angela Johnson (2004, New York: Aladdin Paperbacks). This is a book about a little girl living in the 1940s when girls couldn't play on baseball teams. But one day the team turns to her to save the game (ages 5–9).

My Body is Private

by Linda Girard (1984, Morton Grove, IL: Albert Whitman & Company). This book speaks to children about good and unwanted touching (ages 5–10).

Resources for adults

Beyond Guns and Dolls by Susan Hoy Crawford (1996, Portsmouth, NH: Heinemann).

Big Steps for Little People: Parenting your Adopted Child by Celia Foster (2008, London: Jessica Kingsley Publishers).

Bully Blocking: Six Secrets to Help Children Deal with Teasing and Bullying by Evelyn M. Field (2007, London: Jessica Kingsley Publishers).

Coming Out, Coming In: Nurturing the Well Being and Inclusion of Gay Youth in Mainstream Society by Linda Goldman (2008, New York: Taylor and Francis).

Girls Boys Books Toys: Gender in Children's Literature and Culture edited by Beverly Lyon Clark and Margaret R. Higonnet (1999, Baltimore, MD: Johns Hopkins University Press).

Young People in Love and in Hate by Nick Luxmoore (2009, London: Jessica Kingsley Publishers).

Understanding 6–7-Year-Olds by Corinne Aves, part of The Tavistock Clinic Understanding Your Child series (2007, London: Jessica Kingsley Publishers).

Understanding 10–11-Year-Olds by Rebecca Bergese, part of The Tavistock Clinic Understanding Your Child series (2008, London: Jessica Kingsley Publishers).